Colombia
Barrios and Beaches
Stephen Platt

www.leveretpublishing.com

Colombia: Barrios and Beaches
First published - March 2018
Published by
Leveret Publishing
56 Covent Garden, Cambridge, CB1 2HR, UK

Muisca raft and Legend of El Dorado, Museo de Oro, Bogotá

ISBN 978-1-9124601-8-2

© Stephen Platt 2018

All rights reserved. No part of this publication may be reproduced, stored in a retrieval system or transmitted in any form by any means, electronic, mechanical, photocopying, recording or otherwise, except brief extracts for the purpose of review, without the written permission of the publisher.

Colombia
Barrios and Beaches

Kogi shaman, Tayrona, Santa Marta

Colombia

First Visit 2011

Monday 29 August 2011

Colombia is huge – the size of France, Spain and Portugal combined, and is amazingly varied with Andean mountains, tropical rainforest, grasslands, cloud forest, desert and both a Caribbean and Pacific coastline. Being an equatorial country temperature varies with altitude and Bogotá, the capital, is high at 2600m and the average temperature is only about 15°C. The three cordillera of the Andes running north south sandwich two major rivers, the Cauca and the Magdalena which flow into the Caribbean at Barranquilla. The highest mountain, Cristóbal Colón at 5775m, in the isolated Sierra Nevada de Santa Marta is just 25 miles from the coast. I'd wanted to go there since Ramon and Hans; two of my climbing companions in Venezuela climbed it without me. This is my first visit to Colombia, although when I lived in Venezuela in the early seventies I crossed the border at Los Castiletes in the Guajira peninsula on a

Picos Cristóbal Colón y Bolivar Sierra Nevada de Santa Marta

trip in the Landrover with the family. The locals were so nervous for our safety that they invited us to stay in their compound. And working with the Frontier Commission walking the ridge along the Sierra Perija mountain border with Colombia I must have crossed the unmarked frontier various times.

Guillermo and I fly via Madrid to Bogotá El Dorado airport and are met by two young women from the university's office of international relations. We are here as visiting professors at the UniPiloto, a private university specialising in architecture and business studies. Guillermo is going to assess the undergraduate studio teaching while I focus on post-graduate research. I

Universidad de Piloto de Colombia, where I worked

also have to give a couple of lectures. Ingrid and Stephanie have a minibus with a driver and take us to our swanky hotel, the Crowne Plaza Tequendama, near the old part of Bogotá.

The Universidad Piloto is interesting. It was founded in the early 60s by a group of young architectural students who were dissatisfied with the education they were getting at the National University and decided to set up their own university and employ better teachers. A group of senators supported their action and in 1962 the University was officially recognised. The students employed their own professors and in 1970 the first students graduated.

Tuesday 30 August

We were picked up from our hotel and shepherded to the University some way to the north. Bogotá, like most Latin America cities, is laid out on a grid running north south, bordered on the east by the Eastern Cordillera of the Andes and on the west by the Bogotá River. It is on a high plateau or altiplano and at nearly 9,000 ft is the third highest capital in South America and much chillier than I expected. Carreras (roads) run north south numbered west

Hotel Tequendama Carrera 10 Bogota, where I stayed

from the mountain, and Calles (streets) run east west. Our hotel is on Carrera 10 Calle 26 and the University is further north on Carrera 9 Calle 44.

The University is modern and the street leading up to it has been closed and pedestrianised to form a welcoming entrance bustling with young people going in for lectures or hanging about chatting. We meet our host Mauricio Hernandez, who did his doctorate in Nottingham and is head of research and Edgar Camacho, Dean of Architecture. We go to the top floor of the tower, a huge conservatory that is used for banquets and events and looks difficult to manage, getting too hot on sunny days in summer and too cold on chilly cloudy days in winter.

We are taken to a private club for lunch with the President of the University an imposing man with a strong face who makes a speech of welcome, and we meet the other directors of the University and senior members of staff including the dean of architecture Edgar Camacho, who I take to immediately. Guillermo and I say a few words – it goes off all right. I sit next to Patricia Farfán, administrative head of architecture, and María Isabel Cifuentes, head of international relations. Patricia, María Isabel and Mauricio are all children of

Bogota looking north

founder members who are still on the board of directors. I'm getting my head round this arrangement, where the university is both a private business and an academic institution. Edgar is deferential towards the founders, some of whom were eminent architects.

On the way back to our hotel Edgar takes us via in the beautiful Enrique Olaya Herrera National Park just below Carrera 1, the autopista that runs along the base of the mountains. He explains how the young architects who set up the university installed themselves in the theatre in the park and even had lectures under the trees.

That evening Rodrigo Velasco, a researcher in the university, who also studied in Nottingham, takes us to a restaurant near where he lives in the neighbourhood of La Macarena. We meet at an amazing housing complex near the bullring called El Parque designed the famous Colombian architect Rogelio Salmona. To get there from our hotel all we have to do is walk uphill through the Parque de la Independencia past the Plaza de Toros (bullring). The flats are amazing. Soaring curving forms in soft red brick, Salmona's signature material, with horizontal aluminium windows, deep balconies and views to die

El Parque housing by Arq, Rogelio Salmona

for they look a very desirable place to live. But Rodrigo says the rich have moved north to get away from the violence and crime and this whole area is on the way up again after a period of decline. We climb a steep street towards the mountain and over dinner Rodrigo tells us about the company he is forming to design and make brise-soleil systems, how he's having difficulty finishing his PhD and how his passion is really photography.

Wednesday 31 August
In the morning I give my lecture entitled 'People and Design'. It's all about surveying user design preferences and based on the many studies and surveys I've done over the years. I've given it before a few times but the problem is that Edgar insists I give it in Spanish which is very rusty and I don't know all the vocabulary. But it goes well and I get lots of questions. The lecture finishes with me telling them about how we chose a colour scheme for Leveret Croft, our home in Derbyshire. I say how architects are notoriously bad a choosing colours and often fall back on white for everything. I also say how this can be a source of contention between married couples and how to resolve this. I

Lecture on 'People and Design'

devised a survey. We started like most couples and chose colours we liked from a couple of colour charts. Then we bought 20 or so match pots and painted coloured squares in pairs on the various walls. Then I devised a questionnaire and my wife and I independently marked pairs we liked in both daylight and electric light. Then all we had to do was buy the colour combinations we both liked, employ a painter and live happily every after. This story never fails to gain an appreciative laugh from my student audiences and is the only part of my lecture they remember. I give a second lecture in the afternoon about a project on regeneration in Burnley and Luton I did for CABE.

Thursday 1 September
The day was spent listening to course coordinators and research project leaders. We began with a proposal to start a Masters in Architecture programme and Angelica Camargo Sierra gave us an overview. It will be a part-time two-year course with an intake initially of just 20 students, she said. There will be 5 lines of enquiry responding, to the interests and expertise of the various members of staff involved in the programme. On the face of it I

Leveret Croft newly painted

thought that having five separate lines of enquiry seemed an inefficient use of staff resources and with such a small student intake may not be cost effective.

Claudio Varini presented his ideas about sustainability and Intervention in the community. It sounded ambitious. It wasn't clear if the course would focus at the building scale or would encompass the urban and regional, nor was it clear from what he said, whether the focus was technical or a socio-economic. I thought that this lack of definition might be confusing for students. I was asked my opinion and suggested he begin with a much simpler programme that responded more closely to the experience and interests of the staff involved and provided a clearer offer to the students.

There was no description of the masters course would be organised, no idea about the balance between group and individual work, or of the mix of taught units and project work. I recommended that attention be given to planning the course, focusing on devising a set of lectures and group workshop topics that would attract students and produce interesting publishable research that could feed into a PhD programme.

Liana Clavijo presented an overview of proposals for a research programme in the university and introduced 7 speakers. The main issue facing the development of a programme of research seemed to resolve the conflict between three different objectives, namely that the research contribute to teaching, improve the processes of the construction sector and the quality of built environment and finally enhance the academic standing of the University and specifically raising its research rating from C to B. In an ideal world each research project would meet all three objectives. Often projects don't meet any of them. I suggested that in future project proposals should describe which of these three objectives they aimed to meet.

Research in departments of architecture is of two different types: research that accompanies a design project and is characterised by its speed, practicality and lack of academic standing and published output and research that is conducted over a longer period and has an academic output. I suggested that there was a lack of clarity between the two types of research that may help explain why some project descriptions lacked focus and intellectual rigour.

The proposed research structure was complex and I suggested it might be useful to represent it on the university website and that the discipline of having to describe the structure to an outside audience might be helpful.

Any research programme needs to address three key issues: funding, staff resources and publication. I said that I felt that only one of the camps of enquiry, namely Tecnologia Expresiva, met this requirement adequately. Rodrigo's presentation was particularly strong. With remarkable clarity and succinctness it described a programme of dissemination and publication, links with industry and potential clients and funders and plans for integrating knowledge with pre and post-graduate teaching programmes. The other presentations didn't place much emphasis on dissemination and academic publication and there was a tendency in some schools of architecture to favour publishing designed to impress ones peers rather than communicate knowledge or inform the public or potential clients. I suggested that project teams focus their proposals on delivering both academic publication and public dissemination.

Overall I was impressed by the energy and intelligence of the presenters and how people seemed to be pulling together. There was, however, a noticeable gap between the rhetoric and what I imagined the research would deliver in practice. I didn't feel that this was necessarily a fault of the project team but might be an exaggerated attempt to justify its place in the overall research programme. Finally in the afternoon there were presentations on four existing research projects: work in Cazucha, a barrio of Bogotá by Maria Ximena, Parque el Tunal by Walter, Guapi by Ivan Mauricio and post disaster shelter by Sara Luciani. The projects all had a social dimension, and were chosen perhaps to match my expertise. They were all interesting, challenging and worthwhile topics and the work presented was of a very high standard. I was impressed both by the amount that had been achieved and by the involvement of students in practical real-world design problems that address pressing social issues in Colombia. I wondered if there was scope though for improving the intellectual rigour and, as a consequence, the potential impact of these projects, both at a practical level and in terms of academic publication.

By way of illustration I focused on the Cazucha project. Maria Ximena described how the aim of the project was to involve architectural students in an architectural project that would improve the lives of the residents. Maria began by explaining that improving the bio-climatic performance of the houses would have an impact on the well-being of residents. The project focused on six particular homes and businesses. Maria said it would cost about US$800 to remodel each house and initially was trying to raise US$1,500 to kick-start the project.

What was most commendable was that the project involved students in analysing the problems the city's expansion and in devising ways of improving these new areas. There seemed to be two parts to the research: an analysis of the problems of these marginal areas and a detailed case study of 5 homes and bakery. I thought this combination of community wide analysis and detailed mini-case study was an excellent methodological decision.

Maria described how she was working with the women household heads of the barrio that she'd met through the Fundación de Mujeres, a women's neighbourhood organisation. Working with the women she said they had defined the following priorities: public open space to encourage casual encounter, road maintenance, a second high school and basic sanitary improvement. Houses have electricity and water that people pay for, but in general the structure is poor and the homes lacks adequate ventilation. Residents also mentioned reducing of pollution from a neighbouring quarry and better job prospects.

However, the project illustrated the key point I had tried to make in my lecture that it is better to start design research with a good question than a research hypothesis. Maria Ximena had described how the project began

Barrio San Rafael,

with the hypothesis that "improving the bio-climatic performance of people's homes will have a dramatic effect on behaviour and well-being". I wondered if it might have been better to have started with a question, for example: "what practical interventions would have the an impact on improving the living conditions of these families." This wider question might lead naturally to bio-climatic improvements but the main advantage would be that you aren't trapped into trying to prove or defend an impossible hypothesis.

Maria Ximena then described how an analysis of the current situation in Cazuca had identified two issues: land title and poor physical construction. Research could have an impact in each of these areas. At the urban scale it might be useful to demonstrate mathematically that, given the terrain, the layout of the buildings and circulation routes was as close to optimum as possible, so the case for demolition, apart from creating space for schools, medical facilities and better roads, was weak and the case for regularising the status quo was strong.

Defining physical improvements to a typical home in the form of a design brief that both responded to the needs and desires of residents but also to

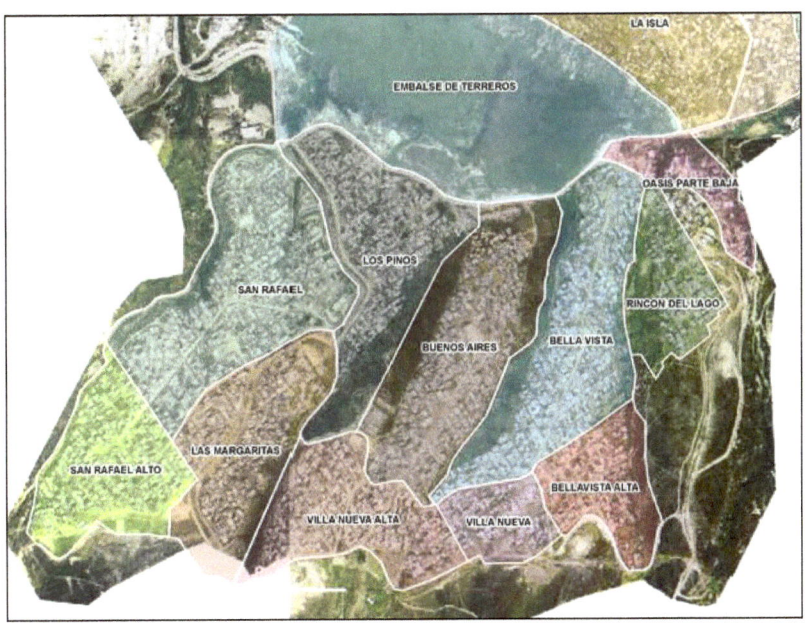

Barrios of Ciudadela Sucre, Cazuca, C Soacha, Bogota

their economic circumstances would also be useful. The brief might include proposals for better insulation, especially of the roof, and an internal patio or light well to increase natural lighting. The current outcome is a design and proposal to rebuild five homes. It might be more effective, I suggested, to have other research outputs: a manual in the form of a "pattern language" that residents' could use to improve the dwellings themselves and an urban plan for inserting public services, open spaces and better roads into this complex fabric and finally an academic publication that described the process of involving residents in the development of this plan and manual. I suggested that it would be useful to apply this kind of critical analyse to all research projects in order to ring the maximum benefit from the work.

Thinking about it afterwards it hit me how hard people had worked to prepare their presentations and how seriously they and the university had taken my advice. These kinds of international academic links and sharing knowledge are obviously important to them.

Home of Sixta Narváez, one of 6 proposals to improve homes and a bakery.

Friday 2 September

Today Edgar Camacho, the Dean, has persuaded me to interview for the local radio. He wants me to say what I thought about research in the university and anything else I found interesting. I was nervous and quickly scribbled a few notes. I described how the project in Cazuca that involved residents in setting priorities was an example of a type of research I admired. The secret I said was to focus on what is possible and make progress. To accomplish this we need to formulate options and describe them in terms that the residents can understand and relate to – such as improvements to the transport system, the local environment and security.

I described my work on disaster recovery and how I had visited countries that have suffered major disasters. There is a window of opportunity of one to two years, I said, after a disaster when there was an opportunity for social and economic improvement. From my point of view Colombia has suffered a man-made disaster of violence, and now was time for change and the women's foundation in Cazuca *Encuentro con la Vida* is one of the groups clamouring for improvements to their neighbourhood and a better life for their children.

Inside a home in Cazuca

Knowing of my interest in disaster recovery in the afternoon Edgar suggests we visit a huge park in the southern part of the city called Parque el Tunal where people from the civil defence department and fire brigade are running a disaster drill exercise with local residents. They are imagining a scenario of a storm induced mudslide or an earthquake close to Bogotá. We walk down hill from the University on Calle 46 to the H21 TransMilenio line on Troncal Caracas, a highway that runs north south through the city. People are very proud of the TransMilenio. It opened in 2000, hence the name. Edgar, like most of the other passengers, has a pre-paid swipe card to travel. He buys a ticket for me. It cost less than US$1. He tells me to take care of my wallet and phone if the bus is crowded. I put them together in the front pocket of my trousers and put my hand over them. The journey takes 45 minutes and I get to see the southern side of the city. It's much less wealthy and full of artisan shops, car repair shops and small factories, all crowded together with the ubiquitous low-rise concrete frame and block-work houses.

Edgar explains that there are 12 lines that run down the centre of main avenues or troncal. There are express buses, local buses that stop at every

Edgar Camacho, Dean of Department of Architecture, buying tickets for TransMilenio

station and green alimentadores or feeder buses that reach places beyond the TransMilenio network. The standard red TransMilenio buses are articulated and carry 160 passengers and there are larger bi-articulated buses that can carry 270 passengers.

We approach the park. The station is raised in the center of the avenue and we cross via a bridge. The park rather open still and the trees are still immature. We meet the people organising the day and they explain that Bogotá is a high risk and that this drill is a regular event once a year. Apart from the male organisers, nearly all of the residents are young mothers, many with young children or babes in arms. I talk to some of the women from the local residents' association who say they think it's worth doing. There is a good view of the mountains and Edgar says they are one of the hazards. With torrential rain the rivers flood and there can be mudslides.

Edgar explains that Bogotá exhibits two extremes. A middle class city north of Candelaria, the old centre, with earthquake engineered buildings and high incomes and to the south areas of informal squatter settlements in poorly constructed buildings on unstable slopes and people with low incomes and

Local Residents at an emergency drill in Parque el Tunal

insecure jobs. This means that if a disaster strikes Bogotá there will be two widely differing scenarios of damage, impact and recovery.

I know from my own work that the poorest sections of society are the most vulnerable and suffer the greatest casualties and proportional economic loss after a disaster. They also take the longest time to recover. They have to reconstruct on the worst sites in terms of soil conditions or landslide potential, their homes have the worst construction in terms of structural integrity, the of materials, build quality and engineering. Most importantly they lack the wherewith-all to evacuate to safe places and the resources to rebuild better. In a sense Colombia has suffered a man-made disaster of violence that has displace millions of vulnerable people.

Fundación Encuetro con la Vida en Cazuca

Saturday 3 September

After a rest, Ingrid, one of the young women who met us at the airport, collects us from our hotel and takes us to the colonial heart of the city. We park in one of the narrow streets of Candelaria. There is a march in the Plaza Bolivar, the beating heart of Colombia where people come to protest, voice their grievances and demonstrate. Past demonstrations by artists have included 9100 mutilated boots, commemorating the number of Colombians killed by landmines placed by the Colombian army to kill guerillas. We learn that today artists are demonstrating against recent government clampdowns. A band of half a dozen striking masked women dressed in crimson and black and dancing on stilts caught my eye.

We visit the Gold Museum and marvel at the delicacy of the Pre-Colombian art. The museum has the famous Muisca golden raft on which the new chieftain throws gold offerings to the gods into the lake, the origin of the El Dorado myth. One of the face-masks must have been crumpled and crushed into a ball sometime in the past. Unfolded and smoothed the bruised and battered face was somehow more poignant because of the damage. I marvel at how gaudy

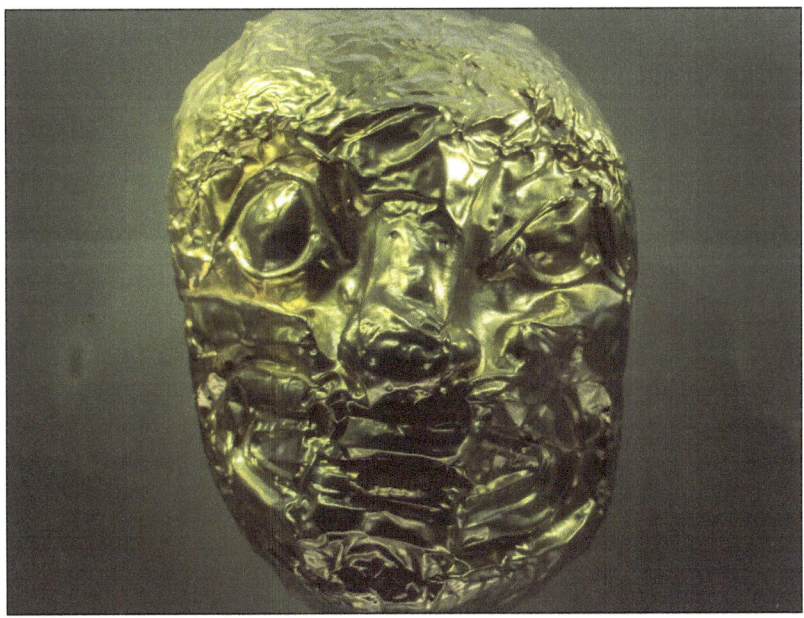

Face mask in Gold Museum Bogota

gold is, and how the goldsmiths had been able to use such thin sheets to craft complex forms. In the foyer there is a striking exhibition of photographs of Colombian faces. They are printed on six-foot high glass panels.

That night Mauricio takes us to a nightclub restaurant called Andrés DC in Chapinero, in the wealthy part of town. Mauricio explains that it's run by the same people that started the famous restaurant Andres Carne de Res. It's exclusive and expensive, he says and treats us. Inside it is a loud brash multi-storey warehouse with industrial steel staircases and landings, full to bursting with the young affluent elite determining out to enjoy themselves and get noticed. I try to get into the spirit of the evening but the music is too loud and there is no room to dance. So I move from floor to floor and people watch until we've had enough and are ready to leave.

Sunday 4 September
Guillermo and I go to Villa de Leyva with Mauricio and his wife and mother. Mauricio did his PhD at Nottingham and is head of research at the university. It takes about three hours. There are soldiers every kilometre or so. The

There are soldiers at intervals all along the highway

Presidente must be coming this way today. Mauricio points out the site of the Battle of Boyacá in 1819 when a republican army of Venezuelans decisively defeated Spanish Royalists. The bridge, the Puente de Boyacá, where the vanguards of the two armies first engaged, is where three roads meet. There is a monument to the Simón Bolívar, El Libertador, liberator of South America and perhaps the most famous Venezuela. He had dreamt of a united Spanish America and in its pursuit he not only created Gran Colombia a huge confederation from stretching from Peru to Panama. But in 1830, his dream fell apart and he died in Santa Marta aged only 47.

Villa de Leyva is a beautifully preserved whitewashed town with a huge cobble square. Away from areas of development this national monument has preserved its colonial character and is a popular weekend destination for the wealthy citizens of Bogotá. We wander around admiring the architecture, the views of the mountains and people watching. It's the semana de cometas, kite week, in Colombia and small boys and fathers are trying to launch their kites in the main square but there is neither the wind nor the altitude to get them airborne. We go for a pleasant lunch of huevos revueltos, scrambled eggs,

Villa de Leyva is a beautiful Colonial town with a large square and white washed buildings

Semana de la cometa (kite week) Villa de Leyva

Colombian style and delicious fruit juices. When we get back to the hotel that evening I work on the report I have to present to Edgar and the research coordinators tomorrow.

Monday 5 September
We meet the dean and research directors and submit our reports. They seem pleased and say they want us back next year.

Patricia and Elmers, Andrea's parents, pick me up from my hotel late morning. They want to show me their holiday home in a new country club development. From Chapinero we drive east over the mountains and enter a broad green valley and pass through a gated entrance with security guards. Their home is one of several semi-detached modern beige units bordering a lake. We have lunch on the terrace. It's very pleasant and the house is well designed but feels a little unlived in. They tell me about Elmers company of metal stockholder and fabricator for the construction sector. It's a family

Patricia and Elmers Martinez, Andrea's parents

Their country club retreat

business that Elmers took over from his father. He was hoping to retire but is having to carry on because no-one is able to manage it as well as he can. He hints that he was hoping Andrea would take over the business but her heart is set on architecture and making a life in Britain, Andrea's younger brother has started working in the company and is learning the business. The problem with family businesses Patricia explains is that too many people have

I ask them about security and they begin to tell me about the time of the kidnappings and how, when Andrea was young, they had gone to live in Costa Rica to keep safe. I've read a little about the violence. Colombia has a violent history dating from the time of the conquest in the sixteenth century. Patricia asked if I had read Colombian Senator and Presidential candidate Ingrid Betancourt's about her kidnapping by FARC. Amazing, I had just read it, having bought a copy in the airport. We talked about Alvaro Uribe who became President and took a hard-line stance against the guerrilla groups, the FARC (Fuerzas Armadas Revolucionarias de Colombia) and the ELN (Ejercito de Liberación). They were enthusiastic about Uribe. We were fed up with the violence, the kidnappings; you couldn't drive around safely, they said. With my

FARC guerilla soldiers

liberal socialist tendencies I was sceptical. What about the paramilitary groups he promoted who are now terrorising peasants, I asked. Murder rates have halved and you can drive around the country without running into a FARC roadblock. And he rescued Ingrid Betancourt, said Patricia. The important thing for them was that improved security had made ordinary life so much better and it had dramatically improved the economy, which must be good for everyone, they argued.

On the way back I ask Elmers to stop and let me take a photo of the city. Later, back at my hotel, I searched for FARC and Uribe on the Internet and learnt that President Chavez of Venezuela had been supporting FARC and this had nearly caused a war. Chavez had moved tanks to the border after Uribe had sanctioned a bombing mission across the border in Ecuador in 2008 and had killed the FARC leader Raul Reyes. But the raid had also netted computer files that proved FARC was trying to acquire uranium to make a bomb and had been financed by Chavez to the tune of $300 million. There was a final ceasefire to the fifty-year conflict in 2016 after four years of peace talks. But the drug-induced violence continues.

Hotel Tres Banderas, Cartagena

Tuesday 6 September

Guillermo flies to Chile today and I was supposed to go with him. The main reason I agreed to come to Colombia was because Guillermo offered to arrange a trip to Chile to investigate recover after the Maule earthquake in his hometown of Concepción and tsunami the previous year. But I have always wanted to visit Cartagena and think this might be my only chance. I also wanted to meet up with Andrea and her parents Patricia and Elmers. Andrea is an architect who worked in Cambridge and was a tenant in our house for a while. She's back in Bogotá on Thursday and has invited me to Andrés Carne de Res restaurant. The flight is quick and I catch views of the green clad mountains, so like Venezuela. I fly to Cartagena Walk around old town walls pasillos, Santisimo restaurant, Santa Clara. I had always thought of Cartagena as magical and had asked Ingrid in International Relations to book me a flight.

Being on the coast it was much warmer than Bogotá but I was prepared having lived in Venezuela for 6 years. I catch a taxi along the waterfront to my hotel; Las Tres Banderas (Three Flags) after checking in I go out to explore the old town. It's a beautiful day and I find my way to the flower market and

Flower market Cartagena

buy a juice to quench my thirst. I wander along the narrow streets lined with colourful houses with roofed baloneys and wooden window guards. Calles and Carreras are like Bogotá but the street signs use names like Calle de los Seis Infantes (Street of the Six Children) and look the same and it's rather delightful wandering and getting lost. I get to a covered arcade of artisan shops with high doors to dark interiors and men working at wood and metal; repair shops, currency exchange, and fotocopias. The arcade is magnificent with two further floors of colonnaded balconies around a skylight to the heavens.

I reach the Plaza Bolivar and sit and rest and watch a splendid mulatto woman seated astride a stool selling fruit ices from a large bowl on her hip and flirted with the customers. The small tree-filled square is surrounded by elegant colonial architecture housing the Instituto Geográfico Agustin Codazzi, the Museo de Oro, the Palace of the Inquisition and the Courthouse. After a rest I drift into the cool shade of the Cathedral, the Catedral de Santa Catalina de Alejandría de Cartagena de Indias. This is where Andrea was married last year. We were invited but couldn't make it for some reason. It was a big do. A service is in progress and I sit near the back and enjoy the liturgy and the congregation going up to receive the Eucharist.

Mulatto fruit ice seller in Plaza Bolivar

I have a yen to feel the sea breeze and hear the waves so I find my way to the city wall. A broad path on top of the wall leads north and I follow it. I reach the furthest end where it turns inland. There are storerooms under the wall here for what was once the arsenal. Looking back I can see the skyscraper hotels along Playa Boca Grande. There are men fishing in tiny dugout canoes, some with makeshift sails. I turn inland and make my way and reach the Plaza de la Adana and get some cash out of the machine at the Banco Colombia.

Catedral de Santa Catalina de Alejandría de Cartagena de Indias

There is a hackney stand with horse drawn carriages for a tour of the town. It's an attractive prospect because it's hot, but I prefer to walk and continue exploring until the evening when I grab an arepa in the street and eat on a park bench and watch live music.

Seven miles of stone walls surround the old city to defend against English pirates

Arcade of small businesses - repair shops and talleres, money exchange and mobile phones

Bakers take a break from heat in cooling breeze on the balcony

Wednesday 7 September

This morning it's cloudy and windy and I walk up the street to sea and lay on the city walls above the Avenida Santander in the hazy sunshine and watch the waves break on narrow stony beach. The Casa Gabriel Garcia Márquez where one of my literary heroes lived is just across the road, but it's closed up. I read

Typical Cartagenian street scene

Cien Años de Soledad (Hundred Years of Solitude), Garcia Marquez's great work, about the Buendia family and their life in the isolated town of Macondo in the nineteen century, only three years after it was published in 1967. It took me six months. I was still learning Spanish and would read and reread each paragraph until the sense of words revealed itself to me as if magically. Never was the title 'magic realism' more apt than in my case of reading Latin American literature in the original.

I go back to my hotel to pack, feeling sad to be leaving after so short a stay, and take a taxi to the airport and I fly back to Bogotá. Andrea arrives from the UK today and I am due to stay at her parent's home this evening

Thursday 8 September
Andrea and Patricia take me out to for lunch at the famous Andres Carne De Res. There are various spin-offs, one of which we went to with Mauricio, but this is the original flagship venue out of town in a single storey ramshackled emporium in a village called Chia off the main Tunja highway north. It is described in the guidebooks as Alice-in-Wonderland meets Moulin Rouge,

Cool traquil courtyard of my hotel

with is bright lights and theatrical service. To me it's more of a junk shop disco with its eclectic decor, neon signs and loud music. The theme is chaos and colour and the aim must be to bombard the senses. From its humble beginnings in 1982, when founder Andrés Jaramillo opened a tiny roadside grill serving it has snowballed into the restaurant that sprawls over a large area and can seat 2,000 diners. Apart from Argentine steak, Peruvian ceviche and pisco sours, there is a vast choice of salads, empanadas and soups as well as any kind of beef. We order and chat while we wait for our meal. There are various birthday parties in progress that seem to follow the same pattern. The waiters arrive singing and present the birthday boy or girl with a sash and birthday cake complete with showering volcano candle. It's all very brash and great fun. I'm getting into the mood and Andrea invites me to dance and we dance between the tables until it's time to go.

Andrea takes me and Patricia for lunch at Carne de Res

Friday 9 September

In the morning Patricia and Andrea take me to see the La Biblioteca Pública Virgilio Barco, the public library designed by Arq. Rojelio Salmona. It's not far west from their apartment in Chapinero. The design is circular on three floors but it looks lower. There are pools and fountains, a feature of Salmona's architecture, along with the pink-red brick. Inside, ramps and escalators providing easy access between the floors and outside there are interconnected terraces that give a panoramic view of the city. Despite the hard surfaces the atmosphere is calm and delightful and I imagine I would like to work here. We lunch in Chapinero and that afternoon I get a taxi to the airport and fly, via Lima and Santiago, to meet Guillermo in Concepcion in Chile

Sunday 18 September

On the way back from Santiago to Heathrow our plane stops in Bogotá to pick up passengers. Just before take-off, a young woman plonks down next to me. I can see she was flustered and I ask her, in Spanish, what had happened.

La Biblioteca Pública Virgilio Barco

She said she didn't like the seat they'd given her. I concentrated on my book. I was re-reading Cien Años de Soledad by Gabriel Garcia Marquez. I'd bought it in Cartagena out of nostalgia, having read it forty years ago.

She asked me how the seat belt worked and I realised it was her first flight and she was frightened. Little by little over the course of the long night she

Designed by Arq. Rojelio Salmona.

told me her story. She was going to her husband, an Italian, to live in Riva del Garda. He was to meet her at the airport in Venezia. He'd sent a ticket. I asked if she had money and she said she had 5 Euros. I said things were expensive in Europe and gave her some more, for coffee in Madrid I said, or in case you have to take a taxi. She folded it carefully and put it into the black backpack she had under her seat. She didn't take her coat off. She said she knew it was cold in Italy. I said it was a nice climate, but cold in winter.

She told me she had been working as a chalet girl at a resort near Barranquilla and met her future husband there. I asked what he did and she said he was retired and came to Colombia in the wintertime. She looked in her early twenties. She came from a small place. Her boyfriend had got her pregnant and then dumped her. She had to leave her son with her parents while she went to work on the coast. Her son was four and if things worked out, she planned to fetch him to live with her. She seemed doubtful. I'll give it three months, she said. She didn't think she would be able to cope with the cold. I said she'd see the snow covered Dolomites from Riva del Garda. It was really hot where I live and we go about practically naked, in shorts and this,

Andrea and her mother Patricia in their home in Chapinero

she said, hitching up her bra strap.

As we approach Spain she asked if I'd help her in Madrid airport. I introduced her to Guillermo and said we would see her through security. She had to take her boots off at the security check. They were new and the way she walked I could see she wasn't used to them. She was very nervous and I wondered if she would have trouble with immigration. I'd asked to see her visa on the plane and it looked all right. In fact she sailed through. Barajas airport is huge, and we found her flight, at the opposite end of the airport to ours, and offered to take her to the lounge.

The gate for her flight wasn't showing but I said that she'd be fine. She had to look out for her gate number on the board or ask someone. I gave her my card and said to send me an email saying she'd arrived safe. She looked lost and afraid and I remembered how frightened I'd been on arriving in Venezuela at about the same age – just unable to admit it at the time.

My last evening

Second Visit 2012

Sunday 11-12 November

This time I fly Air France Manchester to Paris and then on to Bogotá I'm staying with Brian Ford in the Nico Apartment on Calle 68 in Chapinero. Brian is Head of the Department of Architecture in Nottingham. I've retired but we are still close friends. He got here earlier and is glad to see me. We go out to eat and have crepes at Arte-Sano, a creperia up Carrera 5 the road because the Pizzaria Julia, the place Brian went to last night, is fully booked. Over beers Brain tells me about his trip yesterday with Mauricio to see the new Giradot campus of the University in the Alto Magdalena Valley to the south east of Bogotá. It's not that far but they flew there with a daredevil pilot in a light aircraft of his own manufacture. Brian described the hair-raising low-level flight over the site. Brian is a world-renowned expert on passive cooling in buildings. It is lower and hotter than in Bogotá and Mauricio is interested in his advice about sustainable design.

Maria Ximena

Monday 12 November
We are welcomed by the President of the University, José María Cifuentes Páez over lunch at Club Nogal where I went with Guillermo and met all the founder directors of the University last year.

Tuesday 13 November
On this second visit I have been assigned to work on the Cazuca project with Maria Ximena and her research group. Self-help 'squatter' settlements are a major part of the housing solution in many parts of the world and in Colombia they are the main way low-income families house themselves. There are two types of informal land development in Bogotá – "pirate" developments, where the private landowner parcels and sells land without planning permission, and "invasion", where a group of residents invade government owned land. Cazuca is a "pirate" type of development, which was laid out in 1992 by an urbanist employed by the landowner, who sold off plots. Across the valley to the north is Ciudad Bolivar, another huge barrio that was invaded.

The informality of these self-help settlements is both good and bad. On

We park in front of the Fundación and unload the book we've broght for the library

the positive side, squatter settlements are adaptive and attuned to people's needs and changing resource levels. On the other hand they constrain social mobility, since it is difficult to raise money on the capital value of the property or release equity through sale. Eventually, however, most informal settlements become more stable and are integrated into the formal structure of the city.

Maria explained that there are three types of people in Cazuca – people who want to stay, people that plan to stay a short time and move on to better things and delinquents who are there for criminal intent. In spite of all the problems, many people want to make a life in the barrio and don't want to move or for the barrio to be formalised because they are concerned that they would be evicted if they don't have enough money to pay the municipal taxes. Households in squatter settlements, whether developed by invasion or pirate development, under the Ley de Ordinamiento Territorial 1997, can get legal title to their property after 10 years occupation but fear of being taxed means that they also really don't want title to their property. The municipality is equally reluctant to recognise the barrio as this would mean taking responsibility for their security, infrastructure and public services.

Main street in San Rafael

Wednesday 14 November

Cazuca comprises four adjacent barrios – San Rafael, Bella Vista, Buenos Aires and Los Piños. Maria has been working mainly in one of these – San Rafael and we are visiting the Fundaçion de Mujeres today. Nine of us go in a couple of white university mini-buses; I sit in front with the driver and Maria Ximena. It's interesting driving south through the city and seeing the transition from privileged northern suburbs through the old town centre and through the lower middle class commercial suburbs to the south and finally the rancho settlements on the southern fringe of the city that spill over without break into the neighbouring Department of Cundinamarca and the Municipality of Soacha where Cazuca is located. We are taking a load of books but I'm not sure how useful they'll be, they look like ancient tomes. We park in the dirt car park out side the school and walk over to the building occupied by the Foundation.

Ofelia Bienavidas, the Director of the Foundation, greeted us warmly and we sit round and table in the meeting room and Ofelia tells us about her work. This is where the children of the barrio come for classes and there

Ofelia Buendia, direcor of the Foundation, with Alejandra

is a beautiful mural of a green garden on the wall. Maria prompts her with questions. I think it was largely for my benefit, to help me understand better what life is like here. Ofelia lives in Bogotá and travels to Cazuca each day. Ofelia told us that she had wanted to go to the National University to do social science, but never went. It was always her dream to have her own Foundation and help people, but her family doesn't agree with the work she is doing. They are worried about me, she said, and don't understand the importance of my work.

She began by saying that the first priority was to improve security. The gangs create a huge insecurity for the residents of Cazuca and there is a very high death rate amongst young people. Various gangs control the barrio – the Pinos below San Rafael are the most powerful, the Lucumi in San Rafael, the Amados on the edge of the highway and the Comuna above San Rafael. The gangs recruit youngsters in high school. It used to be just young men but now girls are joining the gangs, she said. The business is drugs and guns. People outside the barrio manage the gangs and local people don't know their leaders. The gangs respect the women of the Foundation but the women have

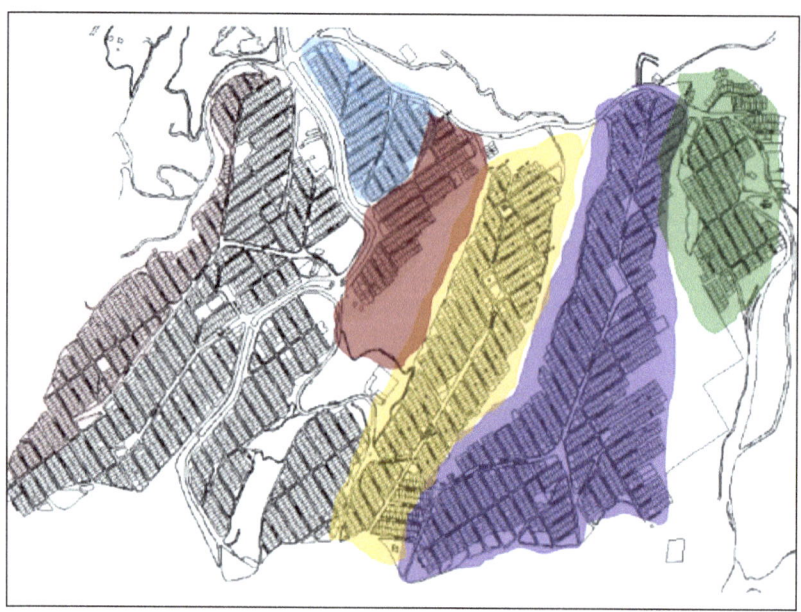

Gang territories:
blue -Pandilla Los Mac; red: Los Pino; pink: Los Lucumi; yellow: Buenos Aires; green: Rincón Iago

to be most careful not to take sides. Ofelia was kidnapped for 8 hours by one of the gangs, but was finally released. The death rate amongst young people is very high and the gangs, supported by paramilitaries, still regularly organise social cleansing expeditions, killing young men and 'undesirables', including disabled and prostitutes, or anyone they don't like, she said.

There is very little pride of place or attachment to the barrio and Ofelia explains that most of the women in the Foundation, and most of the people living in Cazuca, have been displaced from the countryside. Colombia has one of the highest levels of displaced persons (4-5 million) of any country in the world. Few residents have formal employment or a bank account, or receive any social welfare. There is a lot of alcoholism, especially among the young women. People drink and take drugs to deal with their desperation and depression, she says. The big issue is developing a social conscience. Many families arrive traumatized. They may have lost their homes and often they have lost family members – the head of the household or a brother or son – killed by the paramilitaries. Everyone is concerned about getting a roof over their heads and enough to eat and survive.

Listening to Ofelia tell us about Cazuca

Living and sleeping space is cramped

Sanitary conditions in most homes is still very poor

There is a very high level of teenage pregnancy, illegitimacy and overly large families. Typically women have their first child in their early teens and have one child a year after. Typically one man will stay three years and father three children before moving on. Women end up with up to nine children from three different fathers before they are no longer attractive and have a whole brood of grand-children to look after. Because most women are unable to get birth control before they are 30, the situation is unlikely to change fast.

The majority of people in work travel north everyday into Bogotá to work in the service sector as domestic servants or as street vendors, leaving at dawn and returning late at night. This means that some young children may be left unsupervised during the day.

The population of Cazuca is very unstable as most houses are rented so people don't stay in one place for long. Displaced immigrants usually arrive lower down the hill, near the motorway in San Mateo, and rent houses. These houses, however, are very expensive so they usually try to move up the hill to cheaper rentals and start trying to buy their own home. The new homes that the government has built in San Mateo cost about US$25,000 and homes in

Maria Ximena's Semillero de Investigación: (team of young architectural researchers)

Cazuca are about 40 million (£15k), which seems remarkably expensive.

The main role of the Foundation is running a restaurant for children of the barrios. They have a big larder with fridges and a big kitchen. There are two dining rooms, one for small children and one for larger kids. They have to pay a little and occasionally Ofelia closes the hatches when she feels people are taking liberties and not paying. On top of this, the Foundation also provides the women of the barrio with a support network, a livelihood and a purpose. There have been various successful initiatives, for example a tailoring business, run by Emelia, which makes pyjamas that are sold through a church network. Rosa is also entrepreneurial and sells ice cream and runs a laundry that rents out washing machines by the hour. Ofelia described her as someone who was very strong and tough who always stands up to intimidation. Ofelia had to set her straight when she joined the Foundation, telling her she couldn't throw her weight around and be rude to the other people in the Foundation.

When asked about her life, Ofelia told us that she had studied at high school, and although she had wanted to go to the national university to do social science, she never went. It was always her dream to have her own foundation

One of the main roles of the foundation is providing meals for the children of the barrio

but her family doesn't agree with the work she is doing. They are worried about her and don't understand the importance of what she is doing, she says.

The Foundation has been working with one young man, Jason, supporting his attempts to leave the gang and come off drugs. He is 22 and has just had a baby girl. We met mother, baby and grandmother – Jason's mother. The Foundation is helping to build a house next to his mother for the young family. They are also supporting Jason to come off drugs and leave the gang.

Jason's is not the only young family in the barrio. There is a very high level of teenage pregnancy, illegitimacy and extremely large families in Cazuca. Typically, one man will stay with a woman for three years and have three children before moving on and woman often end up with around nine children from three different men before no longer being attractive and having a whole brood of grand children to look after. However, since women in Colombia are unable to take the pill and not allowed to be sterilized before they are 30 and have had children, the situation is unlikely to change fast.

In spite of all the problems of the area, many people want to stay and make a life in and around the Foundation. Ofelia said that the collaboration of the

The Foundation also provides employment Rosa in the sewing room making pyjamas

universities working in the barrio, including the UniPiloto, was important. The Nacional, Javeriarino, Manuel Beltran and UniPiloto Universities each offered different expertise – sociology, psychology, architecture and urban planning. But that there was no lack of studies, she said, and what was needed was investment. She also said the collaboration of the four universities working in the barrio, Nacional, Javeriarino, Manuel Beltran and UniPiloto, was most important because they each offered different expertise – sociology, psychology, architecture and urban planning.

We are given a guided tour of the building first the sewing room where they make pyjamas for sale through Ofelia's church network. There are modern professional looking machines, colourful cloth and cotton threads of many colours. It all looks very industrious. Then we visit the kitchen. The women prepare daily meals for the children of the barrio. There is a well stock larder and everything is neat and tidy. We go outside and climb one of the steep unpaved streets and visit Jason's mother. I can see Alejandra and Maria have a good rapport with the women.

We get to walk around. Ofelia sends Rosa, the toughest of the women, to

We visit Jason's mother

accompany us and keep us safe. Rosa runs the laundrette. Ofelia told us earlier that when one of the boys in the gang threatened her and tried to mug her she knocked him out. I could believe it. I'd watched her, a short squat woman of about thirty, carry a washing machine weighing 150-200 pounds on her back a few hundred yards up a steep gravel path.

Immediately outside the Foundation there is a fenced sports pitch for basketball and soccer. Hanging from the power lines high above it are pairs of trainers that have been tossed there. I assume it must be some gang thing. We walk up one of the streets. The houses are made of clay blocks and some of the older better-built ones have reinforced concrete columns and beams. Some are painted and have window boxes or cans full of soil with flowers. The houses have roofs of zinc or cement sheet, weighted down with stones. Initially building materials are recycled from demolition sites, explains Maria, and the construction is of rough poles, zinc sheet and canvas. Gradually the houses are improved and now have electricity and water, but most still need basic sanitary improvements and the ventilation is bad. Private sector companies provide the electricity, piped water and sewage. People pay about US$30 a month for

Squatters have built shelters in the new park in the quebrada

water from a private water company and the supply is good. However, there is quite severe air pollution from the adjacent quarry when the wind blows from the west. Maria takes me to see the park they made in a quebrada or dry gorge that runs through the barrio. It's rather beautifully laid out with pine trees and shrubs but already newly arrived squatters have built corrugated tin shelters. Maria says they can't be allowed to stay or there won't be any park left. We meet Jason's mother and Maria Ximena asked her how she is doing.

Some house are painted beautifully while other are still in part built. The construction method is concrete frame on a concrete base, in filled with hollow clay blocks and all covered with a corrugated steel roof. Most of the better off properties have robust green railings over the windows. There are small shops selling groceries and liquor and household items, schools and various other community buildings. A white coach arrives at the bottom of the hill and a load of high school boys and girls in crimson uniforms climb out and disperse in small groups to different parts of the barrio. It feels like the beginnings of a healthy neighbourhood, if only it wasn't for the drugs and violence.

School children coming home on the school bus

Sunday 18 November Cartagena

I arrived in Cartagena in the afternoon when it was still light, and after a few false starts the taxi driver found the hotel, the Casa Del Mango, in Gethsemane, an old part of Cartagena that had been, according the guidebook, run-down, bohemian and dangerous but was now going through a renaissance and is regarded as 'hip'. My hotel has been completely reconstructed in the colonial style using reclaimed materials for the doors and windows, beams and posts. The effect would have been charming but for the big blue plastic pool in the centre of the patio.

The room was eccentric with its huge high bed complete with mock fretwork and a mirror, and a TV that didn't work. In the bathroom the floor was constructed from lathes of hardwood imperfectly fixed to dodgy floor joists. I couldn't find the light switch, but managed without. Various holes on either side of the room opened to the sky. There was, however, a modern fan above the bed.

In the evening I walked around the neighbourhood and the old town, watching people trying to earn a living from the tourists. I wasn't hungry, so I

Casa del Mango hotel in Gethsemane

had fresh lemonade and a smoked salmon sandwich in a bar in the Plaza Del Reloj. I watch the horse-drawn coaches queuing in the plaza like taxes. In one, a driver was teaching his young daughter how to mange the horses. A striking black woman in a tight orange dress who had been hanging about finally found a tall American and they walked off arm in arm. Two young women trotted past in heels – one fawn-like with the smallest shorts imaginable. They tottered around a second time and I realised they were travesti. They suggested I go with them and called me guapo.

Breakfast was at a huge heavy table. I was early and had it to myself. Gladys, the cook, served fresh tropical fruit, scrambled egg, tinto (black coffee) and lulu (a fruit drink). I went into town to buy some aspirin for my shoulder and then spent a while in my room writing emails to CAR and people in the UniPiloto University. That evening I ate fresh sea bream in a restaurant on the edge of the Gethsemane near the sea.

Santa Marta hotel

Monday 19 November Santa Marta

At breakfast I spoke to a young English couple that had come for a wedding in Bogotá and like me had stayed on to see the sites. He was an economist and she worked for the BBC and was interested in disaster relief. I gave them my card. I got a taxi to the Belinas bus depot in Crespo and got a seat on a mini-bus going to Santa Marta. The trip along the coast took about 4 1/2 hours with a change in Barranquilla. I had left my suitcase in the hotel Cartagena because I was staying there on the way back and had only my haversack, which I kept with me, refusing the offer to put it in the back with the rest of the luggage. My caution was confirmed in Barranquilla when we transferred to another car. We had only gone a short distance when the driver received a call saying we had gone off with someone else's without checking properly. The driver stopped at a row of kiosks just before the motorway tollbooth and left it with one of the women stallholders. I imagine that the unfortunate passenger would have to do without it that night at least. The car dropped me at the door of the Casa de Isabella in Santa Marta – a swanky hotel in Calle 2 just a five minutes walk from the Plaza Bolívar and the beach.

Costeño folk dancing in Santa Marta

Tuesday 20 November Santa Marta

The hotel was nicer than I expected and that evening I walked to the Plaza Bolívar and sat on a bench remembering the sloths I had used to watch at lunchtime in the Plaza Bolivar in Caracas. Then I wandered down to the front

Plaza Bolivar in Santa Marta with statue of the Liberator

and walked along the promenade to the pier with its ambulant salespeople. I bought a bag of delicious mango slices into which the man had thrown rock salt and had squeezed lime. That evening I treated myself to a meal at a seafood restaurant called Donde Chucho reputedly the best place in town and just round the corner from the hotel. This time I had pargo (bream) fillet in an almond sauce washed down with a bottle of Sauvignon.

Wednesday 21 November Taganga

Breakfast was on the terrace outside my room. The waiter, an older man with a gentle manner, was quietly attentive. The cooks were also nice but the bus-boys at reception were full of themselves working in a five-star hotel. But overall the hotel was well managed and well appointed. The room was queen sized, which meant a fake four-poster bed, but the bathroom worked properly as did the TV, which had a whole range of films.

Taganga is a fishing village half an hour's drive north. The road climbed over a promontory coming down from the Sierra before dropping down to a gorgeous blue bay with fishing boats and launches and I was dropped off right

Taganga

next to the beach. It was a lovely day and I took off my shoes and paddled along the beach, resisting offers of deckchairs and food. One man, Giovanni, I liked and I promised I would come back because his restaurant look the nicest and had hammocks between the tables. But I wanted to explore first and clambered along the rocks on the south side of the bay until I could go no further and then went for a swim. I kept my sandals on because the rocks were sharp I grazed my knee swimming back, having failed to notice I wasn't following the same channel I'd followed swimming out and the water was much shallower.

I walked back and Giovanni met me saying he'd been worried. I said I like scrambling. No, that wasn't the problem, he said, people had been mugged by drug-users and it wasn't safe. I had the best fish of my trip in his beach-side restaurant – bream again, fried to perfection, with a couple of beers. Then I dozed off in the hammock followed by an hour sunbathing and another swim to cool off. It was a really nice place to spend the day.

That evening having had a big lunch I only wanted an arepa, the maize flour buns they serve in the streets, but I also wanted somewhere to sit. So instead

Beach at Taganga

of buying the arepa and juice at a stall and finding a bench to sit, I went in to what looked like a nice restaurant that served arepas. I asked for what seemed the simplest on the menu bit it came as an unappetising mound atop a small sodden arepa and wasn't cheap.

Thursday 22 November Valledupar
I had decided to go Valledupar, home of the Valleanto, originally the folk music of the Costeños, people of the coast, made popular in the last ten years and now ubiquitous throughout. It is a jumping off point for the Sierra Santa Marta and Cristobal Colon, the highest peak in Colombia at 5700 m but only 25 miles from the coast. Because this was a quick business trip I had neither the time nor equipment to make the ascent. Nevertheless it was a chance to reconnoitre.

The Provincia Hotel, the only available accommodation I had been able to find on the Internet, is a hostel in the town centre. It was being painted when I arrived and a total contrast to the five-star hotel in Santa Marta. There are patios with hammocks and the manageress made me feel welcome. That

Youth orchestra in Valledupar

evening I had imagined hanging out in a bar with live Vallenato music, but this is not to be, since it is mid-week, the manageress told me, there is no live music.

I set off walking to the Balneario Hurtado to the north of the town. It had looked fairly close on the map on the wall in the hotel foyer and even on my Google map it had look feasible. I set off through the town plaza with its restored church, alcaldia (town hall), banks and its bizarre zigzag sculptures. On the main road soldiers were stopping people to check their ID. I had forgotten

Main square in Valledupar with its eccentric sculptures

to bring my passport – I can never get used to carrying it, and anyway it seems an unnecessary risk carrying it when one could get mugged. So I cut right down a side street towards the river thinking there might be a walk along the riverbank. The road was unmade and this was obviously a poorer barrio. Maybe this was a mistake I'm thinking.

I stopped to talk to a friendly looking man who told me that there was no way through and that I should go back to the road and get a taxi, as it was too far to walk anyway and very unsafe. Climbing back I passed a taxi and he offered to take me. His four-year-old nephew was in the front seat. The man told him to go and get his trousers on and he would take him. The little boy sped off like the wind forgetting his flip-flops and in his haste. The driver was a young fit guy who asked me why I was in the Barrio and was I visiting friends. I explained I had been just trying to get the Balneario when I'd seen the police and not having ID I'd skipped down here. He said I shouldn't wander around – it was dangerous.

He took me to Balneario, which was deserted. I paid and got out and was wondering how to get back in the dark when it occurred to me to invite

Gorge in Valledupar

him to stay and have a drink. He said he was thinking the same thing but he wouldn't drink because he was a Christian. We walked down to the river and sat on the boulders and looked at the stream in the fading light. He showed me a photo of his American girlfriend. She looked quite a bit older than him but good-looking and Latin. He said she was taking him to America. He seemed pleased at the idea and proud of her. This phone he said was hers. I've been using mine as a camera, I said, getting it out and taking his photo. They'll kill you for that, he said matter-of-factly, there are plenty of drug addicts.

It got dark and he drove me to the bridge on the main road where we could see the gorge and a man fishing on a rocky promontory. There were groups of chilly looking young people trying to hail a taxi. There was lightning and thunder and suddenly began to rain heavily. I was really glad I'd asked the taxi driver to stay with me. He told me about a place that sold great arepas and offered to take me. He ordered the full works for me without giving me a chance to decide and went off to take a couple of fares home while I ate. I found I couldn't face the overstocked arepa because of the smell so asked them to wrap it and so I could take it with me. The juice, however, tomate de arbol, was delicious.

Soft cheese maker Santa Marta

This was obviously a very popular place but tonight business was slow because of the rain and there were many more waiters than clients. The road was now a river and motorbikes and scooters negotiated it like jet skis. A man arrived with dozens of plastic bags piled on his scooter bringing in supplies. Dressed in jeans and T-shirt he seemed completely oblivious to the rain. It was warmer course and once he was soaked what did it matter. He lifted the seat and pulled out more bags like a magician. As the rain eased off more customers began to arrive on scooters and in cars. One waitress seemed to be the maître d' greeting customers at the roadside and taking orders. It was all very slick. The taxi man came back after half an hour or so and asked how I'd like the arepa. Fantastic I told him. It's such good value, he said honking merrily at knots of people still waiting in the rain to get home.

Yuluka Lodge Tayrona

Friday 23 November Yuluka Lodge Tayrona

The card machine wouldn't work in the hotel, so I had to find a bank. I've been told the bus to Santa Marta left at 7am. In the event I needn't have worried because the first bus didn't go to till 8.30. The boy in the hotel was sweet and I regretted being sarcastic about his machine not working. The Costa Linea coach was luxurious and the drive-through lush pasture land was effortless and I got to the terminal in good time in Santa Marta and tried to find a taxi driver that knew how to get to the Eco Lodge Yuluka. I showed my booking. com printout to a driver who stared at it intently. He obviously wanted the fare but didn't have a clue where to go. After wrenching the page back three or four times between drivers, an older more intelligent driver realised that it was on the main road to Riohacha about 28 km from town and offered to take me there for about £20. We stopped at a petrol station for me to get more cash and to ask the way.

The Yuluka lodge is built in a stream-bed incorporating the huge, egg shaped rocks into the design and structure of the garden and each building. There is a main reception with a second story home for the owner's family and a

My room balcony in Yuluka Lodge Tayrona

kitchen and dining area around a pool full of laughing children. Rising up the quebrada are a series of round thatched lodges connected by a steep winding path. The buildings are of timber palm thatch in the style of the country. It's all very natural well conceived and managed. The man seems to have been here a while, maybe 20 years, and his young wife about nine. He is the designer and she runs the business. They seem a good team. There are workmen constructing a new restaurant over and around the rocks, cutting the thick floorboards to fit around the boulders.

Nellys, the wife, has two or three small children and after lunch she offers to drive me to the Playa de Cocos, about 15 minutes down the road. She drops me at a shack in a grove of coconut palms and I walk to the beach, which is deserted but for a couple of dugouts. There are fishermen far out and past the surf in their fragile craft. I walk a ways down the beach but the skies darken and it looks like rain, so I turned back and sit in the sand and watch two young men lever their heavy ungainly craft up the steep beach, taking it in turns to push one end while the other tries to anchor the other end by sitting on it. I think there will ever make it but finally after 10 or so revolutions they tip it over the

Cañaveral beach, Tayrona National Park

top of the tide mark onto the flat of the beach and birth it. It begins to rain and I take shelter under the porch of the shack and ring Nellys to come and get me. My room is huge with massive bed big enough three under a thatch ceiling. Outside there is a covered balcony with a hammock and outside a stone line bath and shower. It's all very well done.

Saturday 24 November Tayrona National Park
I have asked Nellys if she can fix it for me to go to Pueblito where she says there is a Kogi village, but with the rain I find out next morning that the steep path will not be passable. So I decide to walk into the Tyrona Park and walk along the beaches. Nellys' husband drops me at the park entrance and I pay about £10 for an entrance ticket. A battered bussetta takes me the first couple of miles along the asphalted road and then it's an hour's walk through forest on wooden walkways. There is a spectacular view down to a sandy cove. I've been warned not to swim here because of the surf, but a couple of lads are surfing in the heavy sea.

I reach Arrecifes and stop at a beach restaurant and chat to a couple of

Split rock at Arrecifes beach

young women and have a limonada to cool off before venturing onto the beach. It was idyllic and I walked along until I reached a huge split boulder. I stopped and stripped off to my underwear to sunbathe. People passed me going on to further beaches some with packs were obviously planning to spend the weekend here. Like yesterday the sky in the distance darkened and I decided to head back. I stopped and chatted with a man selling ice cream out of an insulated picnic box at the viewing point. I bought an ice-lolly to quench my thirst. He said he lived in Santa Marta and had been coming here every day for some years. He said it was quieter now that it had been but that there were many who still didn't want to work preferred to steal. He asked me about the economic situation in Europe and told me that there was a storm coming and that there was quicker way back to the entrance if I ignored the sign 'saying no way through dangerous slippery rocks'. The short-cut would take me via the beautiful beach we could see below. So I reversed my steps and clambered down the rocks.

The lads surfing pointed the way through the through the mangroves and I reached rest area with cabins, restaurants and washed the sand off and put

Parque Natural Tayrona

my sandals back on. As I was passing the kitchen I saw a Kogi sitting chatting to the staff. Rather hesitantly I went and asked the cook if it would be all right to introduce myself. He said sure and waved me in. The Kogi, a strikingly handsome man in full white regalia with his white knitted hat, introduced himself as Cesare and said he lived in the park. I asked him about going to visit the Kogi village and he said it could be arranged but I would need to give warning of my visit a week in advance and it would be better if I said I was coming to study, rather than just for tourism. He gave me the name of the main village where I could contact Mama, shaman or spiritual leaders who would decide if I would be permitted to visit. He said I could write an email and took my phone and wrote the address for me on my notes page. I was impressed – he spoke perfect Spanish could obviously read and write unlike many others here. He said it was best to go in from Valledupar so it wasn't such a bad idea to have gone there. It started raining heavily so we said goodbye. I was glad I brought my brolly. It was raining heavily as I walked to where the bus had dropped me but the umbrella kept me fairly dry. There were four busettas waiting and one took me immediately. Back at the lodge I changed quickly and bid my goodbyes and hailed a bus on the main road.

Arrecifes, Tayrona

The bus drivers really fancy themselves as racing drivers and it's quite an art keeping the rattling heap on the road and stopping to pick up passengers wherever. A sidekick manages the door and takes the money. People get on with bags of produce, which is stored behind the front seat. A couple merry women got on selling homemade Arequipa and crackers. The young woman next to me said they were fine but I had to be careful – people stole food and drink with a drug that put you to sleep then they stole your stuff. She also said people used the drug to make you compliant. They waft of cloth in front of your face, she said, impregnated with the drug. It had happened to her, she said. A young man had flicked his poncho as if by accident and it touched her face. It smelt like fried food, she said. He had walked with her and had asked for the silver chain and cross her mother had bought her and she'd handed it over. Then he said he needed money and that she should give him hers. She handed over 30,000 Pesos. He asked where she was going and she said to get the rest of the hundred thousand pesos she was owed. He said he'd come with her and asked who she was going to see. When she said her brother, he said he had to be off. All this while she was entirely conscious and awake so

Cesare, the Kogi Indian I met in Tayrona

that no one would have guessed she was being robbed. I have been right to be wary and to ignore friendly advances in the street.

She said she was from Planeta in Cordoba, a ranching area and told me a story about her young cousin who had been forced to join the paramilitaries aged twenty. He hated the violence and told her how they tortured people they captured with pincers on their fingers and toes and electric shocks to their body, getting them to tell who were their friends. He had to change his name when he joined. He wanted to leave so they shot him. The family had not gone to claim his body or to report his death. The just didn't want to bring down trouble. All this chimed with the book I was reading by Tom Fielding and with what the woman in Cazuca had told me.

The bus dropped me on the outskirts of town and hopped in a taxi and asked to be taken to the bus terminal. The driver took me to a petrol station on the edge of town where people waiting for buses leaving town. I remonstrated with him but he said it was fine. It had taken us over an hour to fight our way along the chocked highway and I didn't fancy going back into town but all the coaches passed full and didn't stop so I had to get another

Fishing off Cartagena

taxi back to the bus terminal and wasted an hour. Finally I was on the Bolinas minibus back to Cartagena, which took about five hours. A taxi into town dropped me at the end of the road in Gethsemane and finally I was back at the eccentric hotel. After dropping my stuff in my room I went back to a fish restaurant and ordered pargo a la plancha, grilled snapper, but it was disappointingly dry and much too expensive.

Sunday 25 November Cartagena
I woke early, breakfasted and checked out. It was Sunday and Gladys the cook was on her own and without the card machine I needed to pay. So I went into town and tried and failed to get cash. I tried a second and then a third bank. I wondered if they'd run out, it being a Sunday – I asked a bank guard and he said it was possible. On the way back to the hotel I figured I would ask for my cash back and insist on her getting the manager to bring the machine. I try three or four more banks when it hit me that my bank might have blocked the account since this was the day I was leaving. In the hotel I looked up

Balcony Cartagena

the international number and rang the bank on Skype and managed to get through and persuade the clerk to hand on despite the dodgy line. He said yes my account was blocked but he'd unblock it right away. So I sallied forth in the boiling sun and got cash easily. I bid farewell to Gladys and she called a taxi to the airport. I was at the airport a good hour earlier than I needed to be, I never learn! They are rebuilding and there was no air con, but it was relaxing and I read my book.

Maria and family met me in Bogotá and drove me over to the international terminal where everything went very smoothly. We sat in a coffee bar and I had jugo, a crepe with ice cream to follow. Maria had my new Banco de Colombia bankcard; all we needed was a thumbprint to verify my signature. But Maria had forgotten to bring her ink-pad. Nowhere seemed to have one in the airport until we found an office at the far end of the old terminal. So all done and I'm off on the long flight home. Luckily I have two seats to myself and can doze off.

Watching the rock climbing at Suesca

Third Visit 2013

Saturday 31 August
I fly via Houston and get in about 8.30 in the evening and get a taxi to the Nico Apartments, the same place as last year.

Sunday 1 September
Maria Ximena, her husband Sergio and their little boy take me to see the climbing at Suesca. Suesca is said to be the birthplace of rock climbing in Colombia. Years ago, young people from Bogotá came out this way to escape the city, camp, and enjoy nature. Located just outside of town, the Rocas de Suesca is 4km of natural cliffs bordering the railroad tracks and there are over a hundred climbing routes, varying in style and difficulty.

Exapnsion of Soacha and Cazuca 1978 -2012

Monday 2 September

I am worried that I haven't finished the report on my trip to Japan and I can't make head or tail of why nothing had been done on the Cazuca project since I was here last year. The reason is probably that Maria Ximena had been too busy, like everyone else in the University, going through the process of accreditation. Our deadlines are next month, but Maria seems quite relaxed that we will get an extension.

We spend all morning working with the Cazuca team of Maria, Sergio Perea, her husband, Alejandra Amado, a gentle quiet young woman who met Ofelia through her church and has been working closely with the Womens' Foundation for some years, and Juan Bueno, one of her research assistants. At lunchtime Edgar Camacho, the Dean, invites me for lunch to me an architect called Jaime Hernandez Garcia at his old University the Javeriano. It's just down the road so we walk. His area is low-income peripheral settlements and community participation and Edgar generously thinks I would be interested to meet him and talk about Cazuca. In the afternoon there are meetings with Liliana Clavijo, Research Coordinator, and Mauricio, Head of Research.

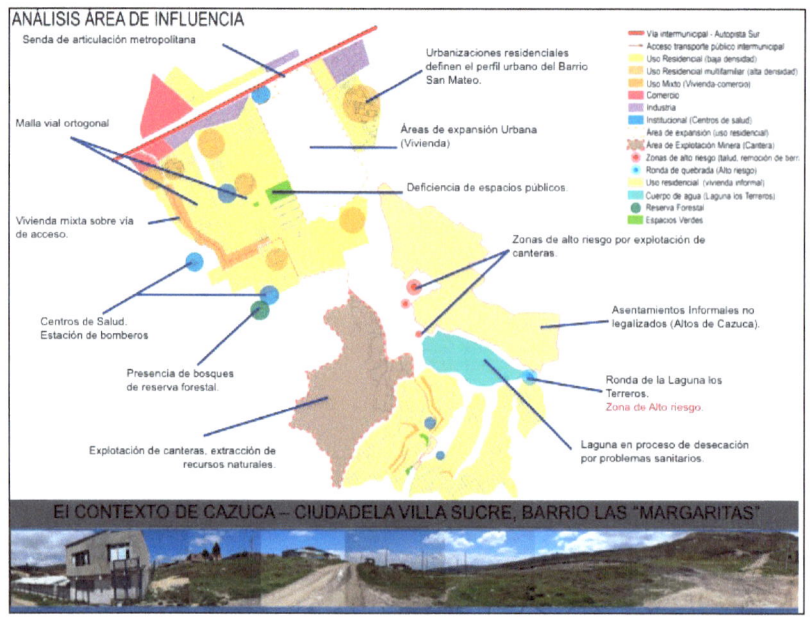

Cazuca context

Tuesday 3 September

We continue working on Cazuca. A question underpins the work of the UniPiloto in Cazuca, namely 'what interventions might have the biggest impact on improving the living conditions for residents?' Our role in the UniPiloto is to develop a master plan, detail projects and seek support and funding from the municipality. My role is to help prioritise the project proposals and test their robustness and sustainability, help write a program of research to provide the intellectual support for the strategy and finally to write it up and publish.

The priorities the students identified were: public open space to encourage casual encounter, road maintenance, basic sanitary improvements, improve ventilation and reduce pollution from neighbouring quarry. The women prioritised an emergency clinic that could treat gunshot and knife wounds and better job prospects. But there is a reluctance to formalise barrios like Cazuca and integrate them into the city. Residents are worried that they might be evicted if they haven't got sufficient income to pay the tax and the municipality is reluctant to recognise the barrios because it would mean taking responsibility for law and order and committing major expenditure.

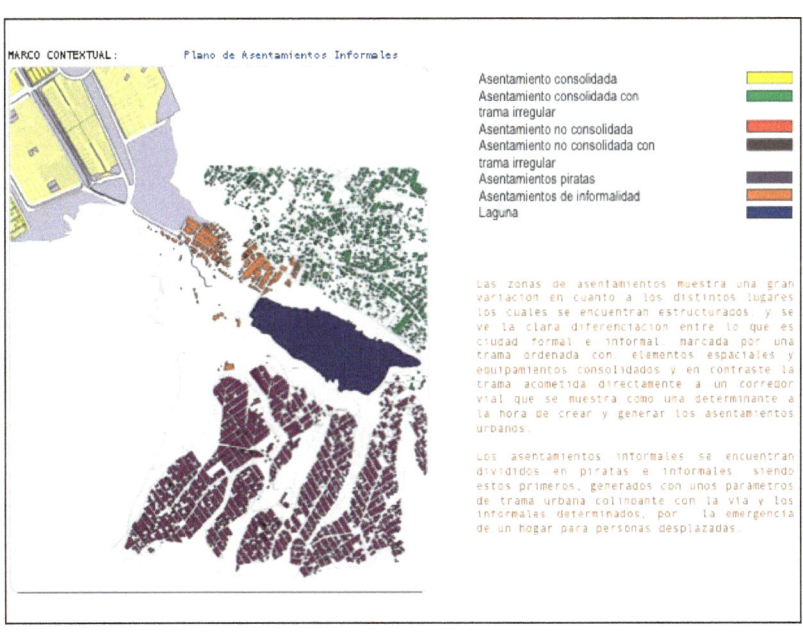

Development Types   Purple: Pirate - Ciudala Sucre; Green: Invasion - Ciudada Bolivar

Wednesday 4 September

Today is the day of the conference. My head has been blocked with cold and I couldn't think straight. Gradually over the week things have become clearer and I achieved some things. Maria and I made two trips to the bank and finally got my account unfrozen and I took out cash and transferred the bulk at some cost, to the UK. Sergio, Maria's husband, gave me a copy of the work he had been doing in Cazuca with the students. The maps, showing a wide area including Ciudad Bolivar to north of the lagoon, started me thinking, particularly about the striking difference between the three kinds of development – the formal pattern and lower density high rise of San Mateo, the pirate development of Cazuca south of lagoon, with a regular fish-bone pattern of plots, spine road and footpaths and finally Ciudad Bolivar, a spontaneous invasion with a much more chaotic pattern of development.

Maria starting the workshop with women of the Foundation

Thursday 5 September
Maria, Sergio and I met to discuss my ideas. We looked at the area on Google Earth and saw that the students who had drawn the maps had not been entirely truthful in the way they had portrayed Ciudad Bolivar and that it had a much more coherent and developed structure than had been drawn. We talked about how to compare the two areas systematically in terms of their efficiency and their long-term prospects for consolidation.

Friday 6 September
The aim of the research in Cazuca by architects of the UniPiloto is to focus on what is possible and to establish priorities with the participation of the community. To accomplish this the UniPiloto worked closely with women in the Fundaçion de Mujeres to formulate options and in workshops to lead a discussion of their pros and cons and to develop a master plan for improving the barrio. The key message is that self-help 'squatter' settlements are a major part of the housing solution in many parts of the world and in specifically in Colombia, and the main way low-income families house themselves. The

Using sketch maps to discuss priorities

settlements that result from this process of self-help are informal, and this informality has both positive and negative aspects. Eventually most informal settlements become more stable and are integrated into the formal structure of the city. On the positive side, squatter settlements are adaptive and attuned to people's needs and changing resource levels. But they constrain social mobility since it is much more difficult to raise money on the capital value of the property or release equity through sale.

We visited Cazuca. Maria and Sergio must have been burning the midnight oil because they had devised a number of workshop exercises to run with the women in the Foundation – the heads of households, as they are called. They had also taken some ideas from my lecture the previous day about how to record people's opinions on large wall sheets. In the event, despite to our late start, it went extremely well. There are fifteen female heads of family in the Foundation and about nine of them come to the workshop. The women were very engaged and enthusiastic and came up with logical and thoughtful suggestions and priorities and altogether the project felt on much firmer footing.

Looking across at Ciudad Bolivar

On the way back we drove up the steep dirt road to Ciudad Bolivar. It was rutted and potholed and hard to imagine we would be able to drive up the steep slope, but this is the main road and everything goes this way. We got onto one of the main transverse roads that form the main street of the barrio. It is lined with shops and businesses and is much more economically diverse than San Rafael Cazuca. Ciudad Bolivar is obviously much larger but other factors may be at work. The access alleyways to the houses are very narrow, and being perpendicular to the slope are very steep.

Looking down the valley from the heights of Ciudad Bolivar the Municipality of Soacha stretches as far as the eye can see. Maria says that the land had been owned by the family of the ex President. It was ecologically sensitive marshland but the owners had drained and filled it. There was no proper planning or provision for the public realm or public services. The municipal planning office tries to define areas prone to flood hazard or landslide by tracing watercourses, marshy land and steep slopes in an attempt to prohibit or remove dwellings from high-risk areas. No land has been reserved for public use and since expropriation and demolition costs are high because

Main street San Rafael, Ciudadela Sucre, Cazuca

occupied land costs more it will be expensive to make provision now.

I have called Patricia and Elmers and arranged to go out to dinner with them. They collect me from my hotel and take me to a restaurant nearby in Chapinero. They ask me about my week and I tell them about Maria and her team and about the Foundation. I tell them about the gang violence and what a hard life the women have. Patricia tells me about the various maids who have worked for them and how they have managed to get on with their lives.   But they don't think much of my idea about legalising drugs. To me it seems obvious that the criminal and violent effects of the drug business are much worse than drug abuse. I acknowledge the problem is international and Colombia can't legalise drugs on it's own, it needs coordinated international action. Above all western countries need to stop seeing drugs as a crime and should regulate and tax the industry like they do with alcohol and tobacco.

From my reading it would seem that the war of drugs has been a complete failure. Begun in 2000 by the Clinton administration and costing over US$5 billion, it aimed to reduce coca cultivation by half, but the street price of Colombian cocaine remained stable and production increased. Half the US

With Maria Ximena on the roof of the Foundation

money was to for military assistance to combat the drug cartels and half was supposed to go to help campesinos develop alternative crops. It didn't happen like that of course and much of the aid was spent fighting FARC. But even Colmbia's President Juan Manual Santos had spoken in favour of legalising drugs as the only long-term solution to the devastating damage to the drug producing countries of the world. He was talking about the social and economic damage, which has resulted in an exodus from the countryside to the cities as peasants have been pushed off the land. More recently I have been reading about the ecological damage done by coca cultivation in the Amazon and how 4 square metres of forest are cut down for every gram of cocaine.

Elmers asked me how the workshop had gone and I explained in detail how Maria was helping the women of the Foundation set priorities for upgrading the barrio. How they needed an emergency clinic, more open space, road surfacing etc. Patricia and Elmers look alarmed. Who's going to pay for all that, they say. The Municipality, I reply. Where will they get the money from, they asked sceptically. From taxes of course, I say and before they can object, I add by upgrading the barrios around the city where hundreds of thousands if not

Lunch with Ingrid, before she leaves for a new life in Austria

millions of people live outside the system and integrating these homes and families into the social fabric of the city the tax revenue of the Municipality would be dramatically increased. I can see from their faces that they think I'm living in some socialist utopian never-never land.

Saturday 7 September
It's lunchtime and I am in the Pizzaria Julia round the corner from my hotel waiting for Ingrid, the young women who took Guillermo and me around the gold museum on my first trip here two years ago. I should have been keeping a journal, but I hadn't – I was too tired and too busy, so I took the opportunity to gather my thoughts and write some notes about the week.

I hadn't booked the pizzaria and they are full, so I'm sitting at the bar. Ingrid arrives, full of apologies for being late and explaining that she has come from work and had to get a bus. We order a meal. I like Ingrid a lot. She's enthusiastic and positive and determined to get on despite her modest background. The life chances of someone born into a rich family like Andrea are so dramatically different to someone from a poorer background like Ingrid. She wants to travel.

Front cover of our book, that won a prize in a competition

It's her dream, she tells me, to travel around Europe con mochilla, with a rucksack. She related how she has been going to German classes because she can get a visa to work as an au pair in Austria. She tells me about her mother and her younger sister and about her grandfather who lives in the country. She asked me about the countries I've visited and I tell her about going to Venezuela with a young family and how people helped me. Finally it's time to say goodbye and she borrows my camera to take a selfie. I leave her on a corner waiting for a bus.

Sunday 8 September
My flight is early and I get a taxi to the airport. I spend the flight working on the EEFIT report of my trip to Japan. I have to write a chapter about urban planning after the 2011 Tohoku earthquake. My laptop is running out of battery by the time I reach New York and I find a cafe and ask if there is a power socket I can use. They kindly show me where the cleaners plug in the floor polishers and I order food and settle down to work. I am so absorbed that I lose track of time and suddenly realise I should be checking on my flight. I run to the gate, but there is no one about and the plane has gone. I can't believe I've been so laid back. This is the first time I've ever been late never mind missed a flight. I find the United Airlines desk and explain the problem. I expect to have to buy a new ticket, but they kindly put me on the next flight an hour and a half later. So I have time to sit calmly and carry on with my report. By the time we reach Heathrow I've got a first draft and am pleased with life. No big deal, just a couple of hours later than planned and there are still trains running to Cambridge.

Colombians are wonderful people and the country is one of the most diverse and beautiful in the world; it could be a paradise on earth. But the country has suffered chronic violence for centuries from civil wars, guerrilla insurgency and kidnap, cartel violence and gang intimidation and murder.

The following year, in 2014 Maria and Sergio, with a little help from me, published a book entitled Cazucá: De lo Informal al Mejoramiento Integral that won a prize in a competition to co-finance the publication of books on architecture and related subjects. The book begins by placing Cazuca within the context of displacement in which people have been forced or obliged to flee their homes to avoid armed conflict, violence, and the violation of human rights. The situation is aggravated by poverty, a lack of social services and a paucity of living conditions in informal settlements. Altos de Cazucá is a vulnerable area on the periphery of Bogotá and Soacha, with problems of environmental degradation, high pollution, social insecurity, poor accessibility to health system, poor quality housing, and poor job opportunities and life chances.

Architects at Universidad Piloto de Colombia have as part of their teaching programme have over a period of 4-5 years been developing alternative solutions to the housing problems of informal settlements through outreach activities and participatory planning, field surveys and interviews. The proposed plan for the revitalization periurban habitat of Cazucá, was the result of teamwork between architecture students, researchers, and teachers led by Maria Ximena and female heads of household in the Women's Foundation directed by Ofelia Buendia. The plan includes the overall improvement of the neighbourhood, multifunctional centers of community activity, the provision of infrastructure for access and mobility, and the improvement of housing.

Children of Cazuca

www.ingramcontent.com/pod-product-compliance
Lightning Source LLC
Chambersburg PA
CBHW041616220426
43671CB00001B/11